Science Lessons

POEMS BY

W. H. New

OOLICHAN BOOKS
LANTZVILLE, BRITISH COLUMBIA, CANADA
1996

© 1996 by W.H. New. ALL RIGHTS RESERVED. No part of this book may be reproduced, stored in a retrieval system, or transmitted, in any form or by any means, without prior written permission of the publisher, except by a reviewer who may quote brief passages in a review to be printed in a newspaper or magazine or broadcast on radio or television; or, in the case of photocopying or other reprographic copying, a licence from CANCOPY (Canadian Copyright Licensing Agency), 6 Adelaide Street East, Suite 900, Toronto, Ontario M5C 1H6.

Canadian Cataloguing in Publication Data
New, W.H. (William Herbert), 1938-
  Science lessons

Poems.
ISBN 0-88982-155-0

  I. Title.
PS8577.E8S34 1996   C811'.54   C96-910270-4
PR9199.3.N395S34 1996

Published by
Oolichan Books
P.O. Box 10, Lantzville, B.C.
Canada V0R 2H0

Printed in Canada by
Morriss Printing Company
1745 Blanshard Street
Victoria, British Columbia

Science Lessons

Acknowledgements

With thanks to Ron Smith, for his editorial guidance; to Rob Scharein, for his cover design (a mathematical knot); to Rhonda, Jay, and Ursula at Oolichan Books, and to John and Laurie who read early drafts of the manuscript, for their care and encouragement; and, as always, to Peggy, with love.

Contents

- 11 IMPRINTING
- 12 GEOGRAPHY
- 13 RESISTANCE
- 14 RELATIVITY
- 15 SURDS
- 16 STRING THEORY
- 17 NUCLEUS
- 18 INHERITANCE
- 19 TAXONOMY
- 20 VALENCY
- 21 UNCERTAINTY
- 22 PALAEONTOLOGY
- 23 ENTOMOLOGY
- 24 ABSORPTION
- 25 QUANTUM
- 26 ICHTHYOLOGY
- 27 BUDDING
- 28 BEAUFORT'S SCALE
- 29 DORMANCY
- 30 MATRIX
- 31 CATALYST
- 32 PARALLAX

33 METABOLISM
34 KINESIOLOGY
35 STANDARD DEVIATION
36 EXPONENTS
37 MAGNETISM
38 HERPETOLOGY
39 Y-CHROMOSOME
40 PHYSICS
41 JOULES
42 HYDROLOGY
43 ANATOMY
44 LITHOSPHERE
45 TIME
46 TEMPERATURE
47 ULTRASONICS
48 METAMORPHOSIS
49 VIRTUAL REALITY
50 VECTOR
51 CARTESIAN GEOMETRY
52 CHEMISTRY
53 ASTRONOMY
54 MECHANICS
55 OXIDATION
56 VARIATION
57 MICROBIOLOGY
58 OZONE
59 ECOLOGY
60 PITCH
61 CONDITIONING
62 GEOLOGICAL ENGINEERING
63 ADAPTATION
64 FIELD THEORY
65 BOTANY

66	FERMAT'S PRINCIPLE
67	RADAR
68	AGGRESSION
69	CORIOLIS FORCE
70	GROUP DYNAMICS
71	LOGARITHMS
72	ANTIBODIES
73	ERGONOMICS
74	ZOOLOGY
75	JOSEPHSON JUNCTION
76	ANALYSIS
77	ENTROPY
78	DOPPLER EFFECT
79	WAVE THEORY
80	METEOROLOGY
81	ANAPHYLAXIS
82	OPTICS
83	DEGAUSSING
84	ACOUSTICS
85	X-RAY
86	THERMODYNAMICS
87	INERTIA
88	CORONA
89	DISPERSION
90	CONTINENTAL DRIFT

IMPRINTING

All mountains now he metes against
    The Selkirks: *rocky ridges stepping south*
    across the border, dissolving: blue hillock, haze,
    the brush of tamarack. All resolve
    he measures by the certainty of stone,
    the way grass catches it, dawn fog
    coats it in grey illusion, and talus
    recklessly records a glacial history
    in substance, still being lived. Dust,
    dust motes craze the air: who dreams of death
    remembers paradise, and all the violet
    of shadow: who dreams of paradise
    gasps at the silent sun, brushes past the casement
    edge of colour into the catchment basin.

GEOGRAPHY

He takes the Greyhound to get there, into
hinterland, crossing out of conflict
into winter still, inside twenty hours,
just. With him he carries baggage, small
molecules of ego, Charles Atlas
ads, maps of places where he's never
been. Promise sustains him, threat impels—
court and volley, set and match—past
open chasms, pits, forest burns.

He claims he doesn't need to read the legends,
knows the scales before his eyes see them:
speed, strength, and stamina—the latest graces'
guarantee of metamorphosis,
perhaps: hunters range across the line.

RESISTANCE

The May night's cold as corrugated tin
when he steps off the bus, mouth set
to reject, eyes alert to movement among
the clustered farmers at the station: hunters'
caps in red plaid—taciturn,
no false enthusiasm for this charade.
A half mile out of town a semi
passes the pickup. Already he's out of place,
lost, lightless, cannot see the gravel turns
the farmer knows by rhythm.

                                      He pulls
his jacket closer, biting silence as though
for insulation—listens—waits to measure
home and the rules of conduct no-one names.
In the kitchen, he warms a little, by the wood stove.

RELATIVITY

*As far as that goes, they could have said
anything*—he'd have to have gone anyway:

    PLACEMENT is a cold sentence,
all fixture, without the sea's seven-
lapping chaos—it's struck by pentecostal
absolutes, not littorality—
while heaven, if that's what it is, speaks
a coastal syntax: he would speed the tides,
dismiss seasons' shibboleths, ludically,
more or less, and to be here, now, inside
the square moment, this is death, he thinks.

They tell him he's to be born again, into
lucidity; if darkness bears him first,
the energy burns liquid: but inland, where truth lies.

SURDS

It's the swift lash of surf he misses most
inland; here he listens for the sky
sighing, the hushed lift of aspen leaf
for sketchy seawords to voice him home to shore.
He is not deaf to silence, but to one
born by ocean's urban edges, bred
to brazen vandals storming at the glazed
ground of gold, it seems irrational.
At least at first.
                     Here only mountains
tag the sky; he scarcely hears the violence
of dagger fern underfoot; the drag
of foxglove against his hand badgers him:
he does not know survival till he lasts out
seven days in contact zone, living.

STRING THEORY

Strange: how the twisted past loops back,
massing at the lip of understanding—
another's probe (abrupt, sincere: *what IS
the matter?*) only draws a stolen answer:
yes. But how can he say *the hanged man
in the basement,* the charm of old discovery
turned grey, the dull gnaw of instability?
Strung up, strung out, strung along: what does a timber
hold? what wire, line, twine, thin
cord of catgut chalks incessantly
the child's cradle? how does he say the tense
burden, touch base with cold death,
and sing in the heartstrong voice they want to hear
their own severe and high and hobbled melodies?

NUCLEUS

Yet quickly the farm becomes a second home.
Acres of space and chickens surround them
and in his mind the world extends—oh as far
as Ainsworth one way, Arrow Creek the other,
and down on the Flats the brown Kootenay sweeps
silently north, out of Foreign, mysterious
Idaho. For now a centre holds:
surrogate parents: one all energy,
lean authority, long demands to listen;
the other firm as faith, insistent as the last
hour before rain. Around them chaos
might race in rings, and still they hold
the shape of life between them, dusk and dawn,
chase and future, otherworlds and wings.

INHERITANCE

In loco parentis: well, they'd have
to be crazy to have him here, wouldn't they—
but they're the only ones he's got—the others,
real and absent, drift somewhere else
in fog and warm beer, and what's he got
from *them* besides anger—*self-pity*:
crazy to have him at all—though here he's learning
air, earnest, laughter: funny to think
he's never laughed before except to
ridicule, or doesn't he remember—wanting
hurts, the cold afterhand of captive
hunger—making the unreal better, fixed
in place at least, for the time being: acquired
roots, a working legacy of summer sun.

TAXONOMY

He learns the neighbour farms by rote,
tabulating men by crop and character—
Old Wechsel's hermit stalks, an acre in retreat;
narrow Cooper, strapped for gentleness,
except toward his dairyherd and daughters;
Orest Myshkin's Madawaska berry rows;
Jack Ratigan's white-gabled cottage,
neat in a clearing of trees: Valiant, McIntosh,
Byng. Better, he knows their offspring:
tow-headed, red and freckled, brown and dark-eyed,
all of an age, all gangly as weeds,
yet marked already by the lineaments of place:
lean, hale, hard, whole, ordered,
a universe of each, a class of one.

VALENCY

He expected the words he'd heard already: *Bad
seed/ whaddaya want me to do kid
drawya a map/ urban trash*, prepared
his radical reactions, only to find
they didn't care about his hair, skin,
scar, but just made space for him,

and he replaces each patch, slowly, pore by
pore. Ready to leave, he looks for a path
outside himself, planting his feet
on fertile ground and finding motion, branch
water, taking land in hand locating
treasure pressed in time.
                                        Earth air
water curb the fire's past tense,
give him present, presence, promise, words.

UNCERTAINTY

At first he sniggers at plain words: *e-*
jaculate, periodic table, cleavage—
city boy, using snide ridicule,
pretending facts he hasn't ever owned.
He thinks his elementary ignorance
shameful, disguises it as weapon
against the rest, the rural, crystal, wild:
nouns he names *other*. He knows they watch him
oddly. Unimpressed, they judge his undivided
innocence, drawing on their own pistil-
packed education, their stock of farmyard
cycles, *time* compounding *Time*, to tell him
where he stands, cell by cell, and just
to stay put, how fast he'll have to move.

PALAEONTOLOGY

The arrowhead in the glass case looks
dead to him—abandoned sign: anyway, rocks
are dead, and reading them is all illusion,
he half thinks, half remembers from a textbook
somewhere. The quarry, down apiece, now
abandoned, furnished gravel for the road
extension once; now it's half full
of water, and they swim there sometimes—
dunk each other against the early heat.
Under the surface, in tangle of legs
and glacial till, he sees filaments of white
stone, the lost script of fern and skeleton—
yet thinks erratically of chiselled flint:
the life and death of storybooks, the flight of kings.

ENTOMOLOGY

It bugs him the way Jack Ratigan can't
ever forget what brought him here, and yet
the white cottage and the country roses
represent a covert dream of safety:
he admires, even envies—then recoils
every time Jack Ratigan's lower
lip curls in clear contempt, spitbug
in stinging nettle, weevil in corn, rolled
peachleaf in the pupa stage. Ratigan
speaks asides, and when his teeth show,
hen's-eyes narrow into traps: spider,
parlour-mad with judgment, preconception,
though quartermoons might fly by arbornight
and angry angels abdicate the day.

ABSORPTION

Feet in the air, lying on the top bunk,
he's like a giant bug, preoccupied
with feeding: there before his eyes
Archie and Captain Marvel settle space
between them, one for love and one for war,
America's sweet fantasies of class;

he takes it in: the way they ridicule
intelligence and hunger, praise force
and find it innocent, follow the honey
pots of wealth and popularity.

Locusts consume the world, massing
in the canebrakes, marching away
the ground. Outside, the scent of dry grass
draws him; even the fireweed is dying.

QUANTUM

In/*after*-season learning: *blackbody*
radiation, fitfully trying to take
its meaning.
               They had to jumpstart the truck
this morning, spark it out of blocked posture
after a dark dawn.
                       But the light quickens, and he's
long ago past the red burning.

The pickup accelerates.
                  He lurches
against the back of the box, shades his eyes
to catch the rearview mirror, *something moving
in the deep undercover—glance, glimmer*:
pulse triples at the almost meeting, matches
the turning, flash and gone, the purple details
filtered in the bursts from patch to patch of sun.

ICHTHYOLOGY

He learns his way slowly into companionship,
from *Beggar My Neighbour* not to strip poker
but *Go Fish*, breaking bread instead
of windows, cutting decks instead of deals:

he reels back at the gamble of laughter, casts
king, jack, joker down before him,
trading club and diamond for the red
heart, the black spade, thinking it

a miracle. *Go Fish*. He's ambled across
a line and can't remember when, climbed
a mountainside, sailed an inland sea—
and yet he feels naked on a cardboard plain.

Bless me, he mumbles: *Who is my father?*
Where is the source, the last, the hand between?

BUDDING

In the fall they graft new scions
onto old stock, peel back
the cambium layer, press and bind, and hope
for spring: working with twigs and cold hands
he starts clumsily, likely the first forays
will not take, what does he want to happen
anyway—photosynthesis—and
why won't the damn sticks stay together,
rage and aspiration: breathing out
demands the patience to breathe in, and how
does he learn *that* except slowly, tree
by tree? Green, he has to think green,
act for October's April, signs of fresh
growth, borrowed roots, adopted ground.

BEAUFORT'S SCALE

Oh, he's sowed the wind and reaped winter, thought
(12) hurricane, in mind's eye,
and if he's only acted violent storm
(11), (10) storm, and (9) to (7)
gales, strong and near, electric, shrill,
intemperate, untempered, he's been capable
of more—and capable of learning *more*
is *less*: the anemometer of spring
recording (6) to (2) the breezes—strong,
fresh, moderate, gentle, light—as he
recovers air (1), accord, and simple
(0) calm, not the emptiness of black
holes, but stars stirring in the void, breathless,
tides of possibility and tongues.

DORMANCY

Growth slows over winter. The farm
rests, resists activity, breathes in—
and he takes on words, talks tempered
possibility, long vistas, tall
tales. Silent, he inhales daydreams:
speaking, he discovers playfulness,
courts the cold with laughter, words' paradox
and twin; early twilight coaxes him
to shadow anodynes—the whole day
drifts in patchwork—he begins to think
he can imagine future: time free
of crossed staves and crescent danger, open
as alpine meadows, with blue lupine blooming,
and distance calling, confident as arms.

MATRIX

(Like being born again, out of an old
mode and into something else, some
not quite comprehensible
new shape, winged creature, aphid, fly,
Easter chick set free of albumen and
looking, of all things, for old pictures—where
does he come from? what womb, cell, mat,
mold, aging original farmhouse?
whose eyes look out from his? whose
brow furrows in the same way?
Straw strands shade his hair, sky
his eyes, cast type of ancestral
lineaments, and still different, still
different, still different, still different . . .)

CATALYST

They name her roles: chief cook and bottle
washer, farmer's wife, . . . and mother, neighbour,
nurse—though none identifies *her*, person,
free radical in just causes, home
conservative: and yet without her, nothing . . .
All heaven breaks or hell rains
around her, she observes, weighs, waits,
enables, judges—but holds apart, maintaining
separate self amid the blind barrage
of opposite and action.
                        (Quiet, dis-
proportionate to dairymaid convention, works
change: the paper amplitude of words,
the bonding ties of literal belief, the blue
butterfly's wing lighting on wild roses.)

PARALLAX

He absorbs words like ultraviolet light:
others think him *bookish* for it, *berk,*

therefore *cityboy*, inconsequential.
And so he moves between identities,

throwing adjectives at the filtered world
until it explodes *simian, viridian,
parodic, discombobulated . . . safe.*

He pictures Cooper in a blue suit, layered
onion in a costive cowshed; Orest Myshkin
with potato eyes; Jack Ratigan as human . . .

He learns deviance resists mimicry,
history derides his trial revisions,

and words: the deviations of the sun
giving his body civil place, and sight.

METABOLISM

At the fenceline, split timbers angled
into crossed staves, he exchanges
brief looks with old Wechsel, who blinks
against the light, adds furrows to his
ploughed face, and limps off to poke
a bent alder branch into the charred
stumps' ferned crevices.
                              (The old
man gathers roots, wild elderberries,
mottled fungi; in a sudden
move he hurls a small stone farther
than you'd think he could, beyond the black
fence. He drinks, they say, but do not know.
Apart from neighbourhood, he asks for nothing.)

The second-growth happens without his willing it.

KINESIOLOGY

He is fourteen, and standing on level ground,
standing on ground that someone else has levelled,
watching the wind rise—he is fourteen,
and so are the other two, friends perhaps,
turning cartwheels against the wind, against
each minute's blackening, the lightning shears,
against the summer thunder's rapid sky,
cracked shadow valley, absence after
space before . . . he is exhilarated,
large, small, he doesn't know—motion
by minute the world is his, theirs, and upside
down—rain is irrelevant, rage, a sign
of God—mastery seems to him the art
of not caring, outwardly, he is fourteen.

STANDARD DEVIATION

Is growing up congenital, he asks himself,
and is he nothing more than blastula, doomed
embryo fulfilling nature's destiny?
Or is he clay, coagulated till he's
bent, stretched, moulded to a local norm?
Do other options even touch the passionate
accident of sex and cell? His mind dwells
on chaos, laws, and God's uncertainties:
noting medium is sometimes mean, cold
as leering; average is bland; and all extremes
are coded skewed—how throw for difference,
then, the curve and helix warring? How many
times can he choose curiosity, finding
the range is ordinary that answers need?

EXPONENTS

Lot's wife, Bathsheba, Isaac on the sacrificial slab,
Onan, Solomon's comforting apples: all
meet in Holiday Bible Camp on the Plain
of Sin. Authorities expounding hallelujah
punishment and bornagain
fundaments bite their words on Sunday,
nine to lunch. Outside, the hay ripens,
the honey of sweet clover perfumes the fields,
sparrowgrass caresses with the power
of unclear suggestion.   *Explain,* he asks,
*the godliness of vengeance: why is nature evil,
guilt the handiwork of good?* Pain, flesh,
and air: he's torn between the scripted world
and oh, the ecstasy of dandelions.

MAGNETISM

What is it about the gang of Fourteen—
they draw toward each other like sun-
flowers, though all resist the category.
Watch them: tall, short, long-wristed mostly,
stretch-necked, unwashed, and tanned:
clones, all unsupported ego, on a roll—
Danny Myshkin, Andy Ratigan, Joe
Duncan, Jed Cooper and his German
cousin—they assemble phototropically,
talking sex and cigarettes, staking
claims on prowess, drawing sustenance
from sheer proximity. *It takes so long
so short a time*, growing together (add
history, take it away), to branch apart.

HERPETOLOGY

Contest, competition: all the guys line up
to race, rib, punch, tussle, catcall,
praising and diminishing, measuring length
and distance, height and speed, power grips
and yellow arcs on the barn door.
Morning, evening, doesn't matter: all nature
masses round them, feeds them hoarse energy,
raucous generality, raw will.

When one of the Cooper girls sniggers *I seen
the little worm*, disparaging, Danny
Myshkin answers *Snake*, defensively—
but now he knows he wants to press,
impress, another, seeks the apple orchard
straitened, stands, and curls in quicksand.

Y-CHROMOSOME

He is intoxicated with it: flex and fix—
imagined valleys that he enters, klaxons
sounding as he mounts imagined hills:
inexorably he manufactures *mastery*
as synonym for *male*, extols the bush
as *his*, exacts both latitude and tribute.
Masculinity is *strength*, he says,
an ox who sucks on hucksters' lollipops.
He has not yet admitted he is capable
of gentleness, the soft brush of feeling;
vexed, he crosses others; crossed, he's vexed;
epoxy sets his expectations, draws him
to his next excess; he mixes milk with alkali;
he cannot act except he must excel.

PHYSICS

The old seesaw beside the barn
stands at an angle, plank half in the air,
half in the long grass, lodged in weed.
Sometimes they pry it loose, playing for precedence,
command of the fulcrum, nudge and flail, spurning
old weighted games for single access
to the balance beam. Speed and energy
control the field: up, down, easy,
territory told in timing. Earth,
air, they lean on god-knows-what as props
against the precipice they cannot see,
enlightenment and uncoordination,
the pronged hayrake rusting in the straw.

JOULES

How much work do they honestly do, thinning
in the long row of Transparents? Testily, they heave
the wooden ladders in and out of the upper
branches, the rigid twigs they call Jewel
Thieves. At day's end, unwinding dynamos,
they look smug at the circular scatter of debris
ringing each trunk's base. But they measure
output in apple fights: Ball Tag, they call it,
aiming the green pellets straight at the crotch,
pelting each other with sting and risibility,
goad at ladder's extreme, bullring moves,
twist and intake, breathing hard: evading,
precariously. After, they claim to have overworked,
but which of them, avoiding gravity, saw newtons fall?

HYDROLOGY

The intake, somewhere above them, in the upper basin
of the Goat River, redirects some of the water
into the irrigation system: sweet,
clear, soft—though dear domestic adjectives
are relevant as ragweed in the orchards. There
he trudges through the daily cycle near
mechanically, shouldering the pipes,
shifting, dropping, locking on, snapping
the connectors, setting spray in motion.
Sometimes he escapes: down the gorge,
skinny-dipping in the iridescent, untamed pools.
Full-throated, arc-alive: music
ripples through the current, sweet,
soft, clear: the tamaracks exhaling.

ANATOMY

The concupiscence of orchards: Red Delicious
Rome Beauty Winter Banana. He sits in an
apple tree's forked anatomy watching a bantam
cockerel: the strut and stretch, the discontent pecking
at small things. All contact with the ground
contested, he thrusts at sky, the branched continents
above, below him: the budding heat, the trunk,
the flash angles of repose: clefts and contact
occupy all the muscle of him. Bark
is skin; leaves limber, ripen; texture
touches him with messages contrary, loose,
incontrovertible as song. He reaches for the flesh
of apples, savours old orchard order,
contorts himself in summer, lung and limb.

LITHOSPHERE

He marvels that the earth should be productive—
mere mud he thought it, yet it yields
hot springs and eggplant—his mind
rattles for the common bond: sulphur
in repose, the buoyant and the bland—
it is the range that rakes him, the sheer
rainbow creativity that has him
dwelling again on ash and stone sidewalk,
looking for the simile, the plain parallel
of urban patch and fostered seedling.
That clay and sand should mould the blue iris
no longer foxes him; that grass should breathe
no longer stuns. The earth grounds him, sets
him free, cracks open to sustain repair.

TIME

There starts to overlap with *then*,
motion becoming place, place motion,
as though the mountains moved with riverspeed
and each season traced a racing world.
In its midst, spare moments seem
elongated, without origin
or ending, caught up in the field called *farm*:
here, a fixed centre for the whirlwind—
yet even *here* is subject to overturning
rhythms: ciderfall, winterbare,
inundated gumbo spring
before the applegarden summer comes
back: stop: forward: watch: space, he grows
like a pendulum, walking taller, waxing male.

TEMPERATURE

A knife falling to the floor predicts
a visit from a stranger: itchy feet
tell of future travel: marks on the right
fingernails forecast lover, friend, foe:
      the world is ablaze with covert signs and symbols
      waiting to be read, like ashes, entrails, phosphorus
      in water, the brief explosions grand as passwords
      in the night sky, with the stars cutting through:
           all things say other things,
           and he asks for logic, not superstitious
           guesswork about the shapes to come: when the s
      moves north to Cancer, he measures solstice, sidereal
      day (and yet he shivers, despite the heat:
someone must be walking on his grave).

ULTRASONICS

Sporadically the telephone rings but he
ignores the Morse neighbourhood of party
line until he picks out "U": the two-
shorts-and-a-long, for them.
                        During the day
the radio's tuned to the CBC, for farm
prices, Archers, Percy Grainger's Country
Dancing.
            Late at night it turns Western:
between squawks and peeps, he hears the mournful
strains of cheating hearts, lost and lonely
love.
       Mealtime grace intones authority
above this cost and law, leaving reason
darting in disguise. He's left unaimed:

the country words languish, however sage,
and others soar inexorably out of hearing.

METAMORPHOSIS

He's seen the trees bud, eggs hatch,
calves drop lank and lapping into the world,
and yet he's agitated—it's not there,
the end; honeybees set the apple
blossoms, each branch burgeons, the cock
struts, but the old bull stands,
bag and baggage ready, with a brass ring
clamped in his nose.
                       Spading earth, he turns
fifteen, and wonders how to tell ache
from impulse, art from industry: science
lessons tell him only half a story,
mixed genes and measured rates of blue.

He's stronger—almost sure: smoke wasps still
in the papershell, recessive, lie cocooning.

VIRTUAL REALITY

He is in love with Hedy Lamarr on the small screen
at the Grand Theatre, her lips, Elizabeth's violet
eyes, the hands, the curves, and Grable's thighs
that never end: no-one on the screen
has a navel, not even Victor Mature,
and birth and all its bold preliminaries
are circumscribed by fadeout. In the real dark,
mandibles and popcorn intersect—
the innocent heart beats privately; and after,
he doesn't tell, doesn't tell: he laughs
instead, swaggers down the stone steps
into the matinee sun, still at the edge
of mystery, inviolate despite
the show: mentally conning the world, and dreaming.

VECTOR

So he's grown, mass and muscle: good
food, exercise, clean air, all
the casebooks tell you why, correctly,
environment: though random permutations
in the gene pool must have scaled him—
how, God only knows—but what's he going
to do with it? *If* and *what if*: poised
on tenterhooks between them, he aspires
to do wonders, yet hears himself grovel
at the hurt of past, pain, wrong,
left luggage in an old compartment
he still looks at, while other passions drive him
forward, down the mountain paths, the gravel
sideroads: earth breath river run.

CARTESIAN GEOMETRY

    Right, then: he knows the angles, all of them,
    sharp as the axe he whets on the yard grindstone,
    cuts a slick figure at the square dance
    Saturday night, down at the chapel hall—
    where he's back-to-back, allemand left, swinging
    his partner in grand style, Y front
    and cross down, almost a reflex, everyone
    in red checks, gents to the corners, smiling.

What parabola loops out of nowhere,
stings him on the cheek, scares him
white, like the flying steel off a broken handle?

    He knocks on wood. The fiddler's silent. Loose,
    obtuse, he crosses the gaping floor, a stick
    of a kid—and softly, slowly, asks her outside.

CHEMISTRY

One, Lorna, even to mention her name
causes him to change colour, fires him
into blurted declarations of *like*. She acts:
he reacts, red and blue as litmus paper
and just as wet. He grins a lot, gawkily,
picks berries with her if he can, flirts
at the edge of touch and gesture,
flushes if others overhear.
In his dreams, words like *care* and *kissing*
come to him articulate and whole;
awake, he needs a catalyst to say them,
mixes them up, lingers awkwardly till she
places a ripe raspberry on her tongue
and shares with him her taste for bittersweet.

ASTRONOMY

Past midnight he stands outside, breathing away
the day, scanning the broad wash of stars
horizon to horizon. Night
scarcely stirs. Venus has set. Breathing
in . . .
        almost moves the aspens,
breathing out . . .
                Orion . . .

—the hunter's darts lunge towards him, prick
his skin in light, the ground he stands on drifts—
naked, he's overturned in sight of land,
rapt in shallows: dreaming, marine, of darkness—
a solitary capsule from the Russian steppes
traces space across the Milky Way,
its technical trajectory a line
of glass reason on a guesswork sea.

MECHANICS

It all depends what you mean by *amateur*:
nobody had formal training, that's for sure,
but it didn't matter when Cooper and Myshkin
and even Jack Ratigan on Saturday after tea
would gather by the John Deere
and give advice to the old man: *Oil
and grease'er, Sparks, Always the carb,* mostly
monosyllables, *Try'er now,* and after
an hour of blunt talk against *change,
pink socks, city markets, good-
for-nothin' guvvinmint rules,* they'd everything *fixed,*
and the tractor spit and spit and spit to life.
They wrenched the world together, these men,
loving the simplicity of machines.

OXIDATION

Some days he takes the tractor through the long
field between the elbow turn in the road
and the old orchard: muttering *boustrophedon*,
back and forth, the length of each run,
catching at the difference between cold curse
and exultation, though no-one hears him above
the John Deere's two-stroke stutter:
behind him he drags the plough, the blade cutting
alfalfa into the earth, sporadically kicking up
rocks; sometimes he pauses, silent, slowly
breathes in, dazed by exhaust, caught
at the field's edge, in daisies. Red paint's
peeling on the tractor, leaving rust spots;
the blade, stopped in mid-air, shines like mercury.

VARIATION

Steaming cowpies and the froth on fresh-made
raspberry jam: they bracket his life
here, shovel and spoon, and as he circles
in his green orbit, he learns the syntax
of the food chain, grass and repetition.
They bracket his life here, marsh and moon,
the melody of skylight and the bass
burden of old time: spiral
memories collect him, feed a nascent
paranoia: *he is not his parents
not his parents no.* In a green chain
he dances free of old birth and grassy
descant dying. Cadences and calling,
late and soon: they bracket his life here.

MICROBIOLOGY

He might have guessed. Commotion the night before,
the bread pans warming—but it's never until the smell
of baking that he gussies up to yeast.
Awake: it signals the start of a fabulous
day, all gust and wonder, free
of yesterday's aromatic ghosts. Oh yes. Here's
the gist of it: the stink of skunk on the back road,
the stench of cowbarn (*clean*, they said; *sure*),
Edna Cooper's protozoa perfume, up close,
and to top it off, the wormy gremlins of greenapple belly.
You'd think the old factory door would close—
bugger it anyhow: but no, he has a nose for persistence.
Composed this morning, he savours the bouquet of laughter—
devises jest: demotic sonnets, poems in puns.

OZONE

I fall upon the couch grass of life,
I weed, he snorts, kneeling between the rows
of cabbages; *no ceiling wax*
necessary Isabel in the gloaming
by the bonny banks or any other
kind: and what's he got invested here?
Safety, *from yourself first of all,*
the lofty parody that raises him,
little else did, fresh air,
there's a special nullity in claiming all
nature with your future face down
in a cabbage patch: *O-O-O*
you beautiful won't quite work:
the solid sullied weeds refuse to answer.

ECOLOGY

He leaves a lot of things undone, left
runner to unmown lawn on the levelled
terrace below the house, and does those things
that sometimes hazard health; he balances
time and mere necessity, urge
and asking, as though untroubled by the long
rack of civilized excess. Maybe
he's learning care, though still confusing grief
with moderation. Alpine firs confront
the farm's farthest reach: field, fence,
then wilderness. Climbing partway, he knows
the summit's past him: swerving already into
diffident poppies, ceding space to the mule deer,
nudging into sustenance and fern.

PITCH

Sunday afternoon at Canyon Schoolhouse
they get up a scrub game if all the chores are done
soon enough Lord's Day or not the cows
have to be milked and chickens fed and Olga
Myshkin's out picking whether or not
God minds in berry season her hat's
tied under her chin and she's concentrating
eyes down as they round the curve pedalling
fast as a bat into bald conifers all
four of them hurtling blue to blazes Lord
Almighty sheer streaks of sailing eagle's
honour no-one's out ahead until
they get there bury the other guys catch and grounder
sweet Caesar some picnic: hitting Home.

CONDITIONING

He gets used to it, the green hay,
stooking the fresh-mown, learning the pitchfork's smooth
arc, ground to wagon, grows from lank
to lithe slowly, inside his time, treble
to bearded bass in a curl of ignorance
and curiosity; sudden strength
surprises him, muscle eases him
into accomplishment, and all night
and all day he is preoccupied
with mirrors: but gets used to it—inside
his time, he fumbles less with image, learns
to love the world a little more as the world
judges him less—he delivers the hay to the barn,
feeds the animals, stacks old bales away.

GEOLOGICAL ENGINEERING

All August he labours in the field, as month by year
he's done before, and will again. One day
the field will thrive in netted gems,
firm and succulent, but not yet:
for now it's stony ground, old glacial till,
the edge of some bereft moraine. He bends
with others, building muscle on the rock
the plough turns up with each return—

he fills and fills the stoneboat, mines the drift,
each step and lift mechanical as clocks.
The surface ought to sink, foundations open
(*sesame*), but no: no favours here,
no spirits speak except the added slow
sight they call *love*, or sometimes *age*.

ADAPTATION

Oh, yes, he fits in, thinks
he belongs there even; he eats, works, sleeps,
with them; wears the right mask—willingly:
he loves them: he would be like them, if he could.
But gradually he picks up small things:
the slurred word, aversion, sullen brow,
somehow he's misplaced his past,
being so keen to trade identities,
and with it goes the act he's never yet
said aloud. The stage is cloaked in black,
and he's wearing the wrong shoes. Comedian.
He went to a faith healer once, and he feels good.
Post hoc ergo propter hoc.
They're somone else's words he's memorized.

FIELD THEORY

Mountainsides resist fields, take
rocks and tumble them, sprout seedlings,
urge edges back against the grassy
centre, where the cattle still graze
in somnolent illusion. Already the fences
fracture, fall; poppies root scarlet
in the verge between suddenness and season.

He spends the summer days and winter fortnights
tramping the borders, tracing the laws of property
through orchard rows and piles of broken stone;
he feels, not sees, the mortgagor's dead hand
staking an abstract geometry
whenever he fixes a corner, crosses a line,
chaos repossesses the vanishing point.

BOTANY

They determine even weeds practically
on the farm, not by bud and stem—
umbel, corymb, raceme, head—but
just by use: mustard in the pea fields, young
tomato plants branching in the lettuce.
City boys might never see them.
Here, they're weeds. Working close to the earth,
he capitulates, sometimes manoeuvring
disingenuously—urging the Dutch hoe
between the rows, yanking whole roots out
on hands and knees. At day's end, he still
notices, simple cyme among the catkins,
spike in panicles, he doesn't want the same,
he draws on difference for definition . . .

FERMAT'S PRINCIPLE

. . . because he sees at tangents to the world they see:
one not God-given but given to cope with God.
They invoke beneficence and practise decency;
he acknowledges goodness in a hall of mirrors,
and cannot yet forgive the trick of cruelty.
He thinks them mortgaged to their fate, seeking
signs in nature to correspond with hope;
ambition rules his own expectations—
so then where's the freedom: to be a natural
among the sharks, a ringer unsheltered in the pool
hall? The river's cut a shelf in the rock
at one point: he dives out of the current there,
into a circular pond. The light that glints on the surface
bends deep . . . he can see if he can swim.

RADAR

He knows when Lorna Ratigan's nearby—
all his senses flare alert, electric,
eyes dilate, ripples turn his back
and thighs elastic, all the while he's trying
to flex his arms and chest. He does not rest
when Lorna Ratigan's nearby; he breathes
spasmodically, burns for oxygen,
hardens automatically against the thin
screen of cotton restraint. Ardently
inside his head, he's singing sonnets,
meadowgrass and moss rose; aloud
he only mutters *Hi* and switches colour.
Lost without her, addled with: he's a
tumble of barbed wire, needles, pins.

AGGRESSION

They shoot gophers, sometimes, or at least
take the .22 down the hill
to Myshkins' woodlot, where gophers burrow in the grassy
edge among the birches. They clump irritably,
scare the animals away, leaving
bullets and rough rivalry. They itch
to prove their manhood (sharpest eye, fastest
shot)—cock the rifle and target trees
instead, except the grazed edge of bark
proves nothing. Maybe chance. Once
the safety catch is off, and quick firing
pierces play, even the cold trajectory
is in dispute. Underground, the beasts,
briefly silenced, scratch and kick and wait.

CORIOLIS FORCE

Rules one to four: plant your orchard
on a hillside, for the wind drainage;
learn to prune, spray, thin, spray,
pick, store; try to sell your crop,
when there is one, survive in other years;
do it all again. Rule five:
figure out why it costs more
to harvest than you get paid, why
it makes more sense to let the crop rot
and bears come down to eat the fallen
Santa Rosas—*why are you doing this?*
The more he learns, the more he learns to leave.
He wonders why the fictions that they live
do not deflect them from fidelity.

GROUP DYNAMICS

He helps unload the apples from the pickup,
heaves boxes at the packing shed, in T-shirt
and denim overalls, like Sam and Lou
who run the conveyor belt.
                                    On the lower floor,
wrapped in noise and red bandannas, women
sit at the sorter: *babes're quicker, have a
flair for it,* Sam says, *they like
rePARtee,* loudly, asking applause.
                                    The women
toss earthy insults, keep on culling,
measuring size and skin, scab and codling holes,
complaining that the best ones go to export.

At six, a whistle sounds shift over. Sam
cuts the power. The women in the silence
grimace, touch their cropped hair.

LOGARITHMS

You'd think they'd know better: checked gingham
makes sound sense, dry grain,
oilcloth and nails, *but pink flamingos?*
Co-op stock depends on bulk turn-
over balancing the raised credit: checked
figures, closed cases, bare bones.
Why do chicken-farmers buy fifty-cent
flamingos, then, ceramic figurines
for the kitchen sill?
                *(They only sound
powerless, these birds, lids glazed
and feathers crested in a castle curve: eyes
that lift from the box shell—stark minder
of survival—see past the skeleton
one talon raised and poised to fly.)*

ANTIBODIES

Up Arrow Creek way the orchards
dwindle to the gnarled sporadic tree,
an old Snow likely, that nobody wants
any more. Stump ranches tell
of one-time prospects, not even the clearing
finished before it's all over—*oh,
somebody died,* he's told, ashes and dust
and little left besides. The other direction,
*up the Lake, they've gone and built a bottlehouse,
some smart fella took a bunch
of whaddayacall'embalming fluid bottles
and built hisself a house* with no roots,
no trees, only the wind to feed on,
lapping at the nearest edge of cold.

ERGONOMICS

Berryman Myshkin, dairyman Cooper, farmers
by choice and deliberation.
                         The surrogate father
with whom he lives, caught between knowledge and love,
eggrun and appleblossom.
                   Gentleman
Jack Ratigan, farmer by weekend persuasion
instead of the bleak prospect of duty, inherited
land, family tradition.
                 Sometimes Jack
Ratigan takes the midweek bus to the city,
courting anonymity in pinstripe, washed
collar, grey hands.
              Cooper's world,
dour as muscle, thrives on repetition.
Myshkin's needs grace, sweet water cycling
sun.
     The chicken run just survives,
or means survival, if the orchard falters.

ZOOLOGY

So much depended on the red
Rhode Island chickens: life and death, to start with,
keeping the hens in, the dogs out,
the chicken wire upright. Collecting the eggs:
cleaning, sizing; candling, marketing; checking them
under the broodies; culling the hens that ate
their own, you couldn't trust 'em; and an eggless
henhouse isn't worth the time it takes to shovel
the shit out, rainwater or no rainwater.
Not to mention the bloody rooster, spends
all his time on the wheelbarrow for god's sake,
and who left that outside in the first place?
He came to know too much to like them. Still,
it wasn't easy, the first time, to slit the gullets.

JOSEPHSON JUNCTION

Why do they want so much to be born again?
What mad resistance to living draws them
to that world instead of this? What
tunnel do they find themselves inhabiting—
despite, or is it because of love—that
altered states would change? Do they expect
electric haloes? angels' wings rising
damp from dew? immersion in the infinite
blue sky? They've opened their house to him, and yet
conducted praise; they've made it possible
for him to grow, yet asked alternatives
he cannot follow—cannot cross them either:
this dense line divides, approaching zero,
charging bar and barrier, stalk and stave.

ANALYSIS

Bacilli are ubiquitous in soil
his schoolbooks say, and where are the plain germs
of yesterday: the place he *once* called real
couldn't care less about dirt,
but here, chicken pellets and the pile-high
cattledung drive the farm's renewal:
worms waste nothing, and all that was
becomes the everlasting:
                              Eternity consists
in this, he thinks, not the silk wings
of summer angels: to be born again as grass,
that's the future: *rot, decay,* are words
that spell nostalgia: the *process* carries forward,
not the people, not their civil rules:
being saved is *this* world's passing grace.

ENTROPY

Time condenses: the summer evaporates.

He says he knows the lineaments of law—
but cannot work the algorithm.
                              Every
where: breakdown. Measure, forward foot.

No mist collects in the crevices of August,
only heat.
          Each second stretches,
folds out, elongates, pushes past
the limits of sobriety, expands
into a universe, and yet the summer
ceases, ochres, dries. *Then*; and then . . .
              .
two separate zones: flying, catching
back.
     In the air the harvest dust
thickens, its dissipation held in escrow
till a legible hypothesis of rain.

DOPPLER EFFECT

Distant, he listens for the train's rattle
down across the valley—the Swanson horn
signalling approach, blare and past already, fading
while each carriage light electrifies the dark.
He lets acoustic eyes imagine passengers:
vested men, portly with cigars,
solid women knitting, long-necked youngsters
leaving for the first time, seeking city,
all insinuating each other's dreams.
No-one notices the cast of expectation
governs hearing, how the night wind
wells upward, narrative accosts the living,
destinations once too far for reaching
pass unsoundly, blaze and disappear.

WAVE THEORY

He said, she said, *Hi,* stumbling over
the synchronicity, glancing at each other's
eyes, and then away again, shuffling,
towards *You wanna* (he said, she said) *walk,
I guess?* Through the stand of sweet corn,
tassels silk and drifting, into the hayfield.

He attempts to saunter, she to stroll,
he with a stalk of timothy in his teeth,
she letting her hand caress the grass
and then, as though by accident, his.

Air they scarcely notice curls and rustles
each dry leaf, along, across
this inland sea. In shy experiments of touch
and part, they sail an unfamiliar coast, discovering.

METEOROLOGY

When the storm hits again, it thunders epithets,
adjectival blasts and gusting grammar,
your perverted effing kind: Jack
and Myrna Ratigan discard their palace
manners to send him *all to buggery*, cite
the cold day in hell as a likely time
for calmer discourse.   Used to be names didn't
faze him, but he's diminished by their polar
pronoun *That*: confronted, eyes
down, knocking over a sugar bowl:
Get away resonates. He draws in,
from ice *away* the gate *away* the painted
gables gone that promised Arcady
and idly bartered bitter strangleholds.

ANAPHYLAXIS

Maybe it's happened too many times already:
now he reads rejection with the blanched face
of pain—shame drains him of colour—wit
deserts him. He has nothing to say, nothing to lift
the weight that presses air from his lungs, denies
him substance, though all around him mass and motion
dispute the likelihood of vulnerability.

Heartless, the rules don't work, don't seem to work—
the laws of science constitute a fiction,
the interim truth of *not disproving*: so why
does he breathe in shallows, resist open weeping—
only in case someone sees? Outside,
the goldenrod: within, a pale gasp—
not of recognition but of fear.

OPTICS

Ruminant (noun: cud-chewer); *ruminare*
(chew over); *rumens* (gullet): how in a field
the cattle stand one way, facing
the gate, placid, dog-watchful, as though they
always lived in standard time, and knew
the purple light was coming on. Hours
spent noticing shades, and still . . .

That night he tossed sleepless, crossed street
by ashen doorway, borderland by unforeseen,
face it (*basement, ties*): the man (height:
stock; hair: gnawed; eyes: obscured) was saying
Come, I have a room. Quiet. Swallow,
look away: through the glass see out of time
the placeless root of worry, the mulling dark.

DEGAUSSING

Charged from pole to pole with thunder, he's
one against the world: work and torn
faith telling him to build now
in stone, cede to ground (*learning, loss*),
or else decay: he's fire magnet,
prey of possibility—but cannot turn
aside his lessons, past and place: words
like *apple-orchard, quarry, river, woodlot*
lead him, every lightning-strike, across a broken
field—strange chaos surrounds him, not
electric anarchy (the pain *confusion*):
chaos is organized, alphabets
of accidental filings, iron seed: coast
and counterforce of fireweed and foil.

ACOUSTICS

Listen: when the summer sun began
    Lesson one: December will begin,
warming earth and air and every bud,
    worms will eat, and errant winds forbid
all creation dressed in sudden wonder;
    eloquence. Predestined sullen winter;
high up in the cherry orchards, white
    who appreciates its icy white
blossom sets, day approaches noon,
    blast, its adze-grey reaches? No-one.
crickets leap, chirp, chatter, and repeat:
    Cracked lips, sharp shattering retreat.
listen to the summer take its easing.
    Lesson two: remember echo's season.

X-RAY

:is winter's season, apple branch reduced
to skeleton, stalks above snow: even
the black bears hibernate, and only owls patrol
the open barn: winds veer from the north,
drifts bury the fenceline, leave stray
cornerposts to mark terrain: now
there is no earth, no break from sky, the world
is white, with black bones: in seconds, blood
freezes, all flesh is crystalline,
still.   Luminescence: one snap
and motion starts again, the white rabbit
darts across a field, the sky burns
cobalt, sun in capricorn, low light
turning early dark, and bitterchill.

THERMODYNAMICS

Sun, snow, and sun again: *enough*
of this gauging—three years here
and driving the tractor since he was thirteen,
the pickup almost as long, on the back road—
time to move on, and yet he'll never have
enough of *this*: the sun speeding through
the cycles that make him *man*, the sustenance
of light, the dark that drives him. He's not used
to traffic yet, pedestrian controls,
the cold choice of raincoast streets,
from this advantage. He may need
to corral the summer, make it work for him—
a conduit: whether start or finish,
zero's still uncertain, like the dead.

INERTIA

This time he's sitting alone on the back stoop,
thinking, listening to the hemlock breathe,
watching the four cats, or none of the above:
maybe Jason never had such moments,
the Argonauts always in a snit,
Stooges hyperactive, Superman
cryptic—and Einstein: was it xenophobia
kept the second Nobel lost, or plain
anti-Semitism?   Wherever *there* is—
Stockholm, Hollywood, the rest—the air is
paused in half-examined heat. Here
sunrays pierce the conifers in patches
furzy gold: nothing is happening unless
he's moving, going to move, or stopping still.

CORONA

Ring around the sun ring around
the moon: fire and ice—he reads seasons
by the circle that contains or crowns him, solid earth,
charred sky, the canticles of wind and rain,
ring around and down. He's drawn by music
in the odd disorder of the world's enclosures, black
holes and white dwarfs, and quarks that sing
outside the fundaments of gravity—
a lullaby of reason. Roses clamber
through staff, stave, and signature. Impediments
dissolve in envelopes of sound. Charged
with change, he spurns the static hush and hiss
of rhetoric, the heavyhead mistakes
of fixed stars, crystal nights, and eden.

DISPERSION

And so he goes. And God, they say, be with you
(*riddance, riddance* rutting in the wheels
of Jack-and-Myrna memories, till cold rail
suspends their white duress), God grant you peace.
Pieces maybe (how the lewd inter-
rupts the harbour grace: he has not yet
arrived and would be *arriviste*, God
save the King). During interludes
he follows a separate train, savours kith
and kin, blood fact and bone notion,
sees endurance ending, hard promises
a riddling elusive ride beyond belief
or past reform. Prism. He's wearing away
his good clothes: outwardly, and carrying on.

CONTINENTAL DRIFT

Then he is another, and himself, and still
changing: the land drifts apart, the
great divide to the east, the rift valley,
rivers flowing all ways to the oceans—
and he is torn between them, longing to be,
something, not this ragged corpse he half
invents, half recognizes behind
the masks he wears, old holograms of hope.
To be: he lives in aspiration, each
breath a gasp, and speaks in inarticulate
monosyllables, *yes, no, there.*
There is where he would be, at the heart,
while some insistent drive towards displacement
edges him onward, step by sea by singing.

WILLIAM HERBERT NEW

ABOUT THE AUTHOR

W.H. New was born in Vancouver, in a year when the city seemed to move more slowly, though the world was about to go to war. He grew up in a working-class neighbourhood in South Vancouver, near the end of the Fraser streetcar line, and early learned the words of danger and dream: *Timbucktu* and *Mandalay, Lillooet* and *Kootenay, air raid* and *blackout, Dieppe* and *Samarkand*. Large tracts of city land grew wild then, fostering thimbleberries and spear bracken, scrub alder and salal; they served as playground, and as a kind of school.

Later, he met the larger wilderness up close—lynx, bear moose, fool hen—working on geochemical surveys in the summer months between terms at the University of B.C. He has hiked through much of British Columbia—in the mountains near Cranbrook and Keremeos, in the highland valleys near Aiyansh and Taseko Lake—and while at graduate school at the

University of Leeds, he also walked extensively through the Yorkshire dales and moors. He has worked as an apple picker, a shoe salesman, a shipping clerk for an art materials supplier, a draftsman, a water-tester, and an instructor in a geomorphology lab. For 18 years, he was also the editor of the distinguished critical quarterly *Canadian Literature*. Having lectured and taught for brief periods in countries as diverse as Australia, China, France, India, Italy, New Zealand, and the U.S.A., he is the current holder of the Brenda & David McLean Chair in Canadian Studies at U.B.C. He specializes in teaching the English-language literatures of the Commonwealth.

Married, with two sons, he lives in Vancouver. In his spare time he enjoys gardening, painting, and the unforgiving racquet sport called squash.

Among his more than thirty books—mostly concerned with the wilds of language-in-action—are *Dreams of Speech and Violence, Articulating West, A History of Canacian Literature, Inside the Poem, Canadian Short Fiction,* and (with W.E. Messenger) *Active Voice* and *Literature in English.*

Science Lessons is his first book of poetry.